The Art of Table Setting

Also from Westphalia Press

westphaliapress.org

The Idea of the Digital University

Masonic Tombstones and Masonic Secrets

Eight Decades in Syria

Avant-Garde Politician

L'Enfant and the Freemasons

Baronial Bedrooms

Conflicts in Health Policy

Material History and Ritual Objects

Paddle Your Own Canoe

Opportunity and Horatio Alger

Careers in the Face of Challenge

Bookplates of the Kings

Collecting American Presidential Autographs

Misunderstood Children

Original Cables from the Pearl Harbor Attack

Social Satire and the Modern Novel

The Amenities of Book Collecting

The Genius of Freemasonry

A Definitive Commentary on Bookplates

James Martineau and Rebuilding Theology

No Bird Lacks Feathers

Earthworms, Horses, and Living Things

The Man Who Killed President Garfield

Anti-Masonry and the Murder of Morgan

Understanding Art

Homeopathy

Ancient Masonic Mysteries

Collecting Old Books

The Boy Chums Cruising in Florida Waters

The Thomas Starr King Dispute

Ivanhoe Masonic Quartettes

Lariats and Lassos

Mr. Garfield of Ohio

The Wisdom of Thomas Starr King

The French Foreign Legion

War in Syria

Naturism Comes to the United States

New Sources on Women and Freemasonry

Designing, Adapting, Strategizing in Online Education

Gunboat and Gun-runner

Meeting Minutes of Naval Lodge No. 4 F.A.A.M

The Art of Table Setting

Ancient and Modern

by Claudia Quigley Murphy

WESTPHALIA PRESS
An imprint of Policy Studies Organization

Westphalia Press
An imprint of Policy Studies Organization
1527 New Hampshire Ave., NW
Washington, D.C. 20036
info@ipsonet.org

ISBN-13: 978-1-63391-185-7
ISBN-10: 1633911853

Cover design by Jeffrey Barnes:
jbarnesbook.design

Daniel Gutierrez-Sandoval, Executive Director
PSO and Westphalia Press

Updated material and comments on this edition
can be found at the Westphalia Press website:
www.westphaliapress.org

The Art of
Table Setting
by
Claudia Quigley Murphy

The Entrance of a Masque of Minstrels or Actors
At a Royal Banquet in the Time of Henry VIII

The HISTORY of the
Art of Tablesetting
ANCIENT AND MODERN

FROM ANGLO-SAXON DAYS TO THE PRES-
ENT TIME, WITH ILLUSTRATIONS AND
BIBLIOGRAPHY. FOR THE USE OF
SCHOOLS, COLLEGES, EXTENSION
WORKERS, WOMEN'S CLUBS, Etc., Etc.

By

CLAUDIA QUIGLEY MURPHY
CONSULTANT IN HOME ECONOMICS

1   9   2   1

THIS MONOGRAPH is intended to give content of knowledge which shall be accurate and suggestive on the subject of TABLESETTING for use in Schools, Colleges, and by Extension Workers and Women's Clubs, *etc.*

So far as the Modern Silver and Tableware is concerned, it is based on *Gorham Silverware.* But the content of the MONOGRAPH is universal information and may be treated as such in the classroom.

Tablesetting

OUR social customs, as well as our language, are easily traceable to our Anglo-Saxon origin. From the days of King Arthur, that heroic monarch with his knights of legend and mystery, the round table has been a synonym for community of interest and adventure. Great as is the contrast in material things between the barbarism of these long-ago yesterdays and the luxuries of to-day, it is even less than the contrast between the manners and habits of the guests at the festive board. Unless we occasionally glance back at the successive steps leading to our modern environment, we cannot realize that (simple American citizens that we are) we are enjoying as every-day comfort a luxury in tablesetting and equipment unknown to the greatest monarch or the richest noble in the days of our not very remote ancestors.

In all the illustrations of the Anglo-Saxon period, the tablesetting included the Salt Cellar, which was the first thing put on the table. The salt was far more than the necessary condiment as we know it. It was in itself symbolic. To sit above the salt was to sit in a place of honor, and until the salt was put upon the table no one could know where would be his allotted seat. Then came the silver dishes for holding vegetable or fish, sometimes meat, the

round cross-marked articles being small loaves of
bread, always present, the "manchet" of early days.
Occasionally a knife is shown, and a prescribed rule
was that it be well scoured; the spoons and knives

An Anglo-Saxon Dinner
With servants presenting food kneeling

were not furnished by the host, but were brought
by guests whose servants, so equipped, cut the meat
and carved the food for each person.

The fair and bonny Queen Elizabeth was accus-
tomed to lift to her mouth with her virgin fingers
the second joint of the turkey and gnaw it to
depletion.

Careful rules were laid down for the carvers,
where the Officer of the Mouth, or carver, is told:
"Set never on fish, flesh, beast, or fowl more than two
fingers and a thumb."

The guests had no plates or forks and few knives,
but ate with their hands, and threw the refuse on
the floors, which were usually stone, sometimes
covered with rushes. Dogs and cats were freely

invited to all feasts to serve a most useful purpose—
of gathering discarded food. In the "Book of
Courtesy" it is noted as very bad form to stroke the
dog or cat availing itself of the general hospitality.
Nor is the guest at the noble table to pick his teeth
with his knife.

The Cloth

AT THAT time the cleanliness of the cloth, or
Nappe, was of paramount importance and a
matter of great pride. Generally speaking, the
service on the tables was very simple, consisting of
the silver bread basket for the notables, cups, some-

Anglo-Saxons at Table
Early print showing men and women at table; utensils
of that period. Note the absence of table legs or
supports for table

times stands for the dishes of meat and vegetables
(called messes) brought by the cook, the knife and
sometimes spoons for soup and liquid, and always the
small round loaf of bread, or manchet.

Hands were usually wiped on the sides of the table-cloth, for napkins were not in general use. Later came the silver ewer (or pitcher) and laver (or basin), presented by a servitor with towel on his arm, as shown in many old illustrations; here the hands and possibly lips were cleansed from greasy

A King at Dinner

contact of food, for there were no intervening forks in that period. The ceremony of using the ewer and laver (or basin) preceded as well as followed the meal. The need for formal finger-cleansing was imperative, as the food was served in messes or on trenchers, which were the common service for at least two, and frequently for four or more persons. So eating off the same plate in the days of Chaucer was more than a figure of speech. In the romance of "Lancelot du Lac," a lady complains to her husband "that she has not eaten off the same dish with her knight for several years."

The niceties of table manners even then demanded that the hands which dipped into the common dish should be clean. That it was no easy thing to meet the requirements of table courtesy and eat daintily is shown by Chaucer in his picture of the Prioress, the gentlewoman of his day, of whom he writes:

"Ther was also a Nonne, a Prioresse,

.   .   .   .   .

"At mete wel i-taught was sche withalle;
"Sche leet no morsel from hire lippes falle,
"Ne wette hire fyngres in hire sauce deepe.
"Wel cowde sche carie a morsel, and wel keepe,
"That no drop fil uppon hire brest.

.   .   .   .   .

"Hire overlippe wypud sche so clene,
"That in hire cuppe was no ferthing sene
"Of grees, when sche dronken hadde hire draught
"Ful semely aftur hire mete sche raught."

While the nobility expressed its wealth in its silver trenchers, wassail bowls, ewers, lavers, basins and other implements and tools of the table, the Yeoman gloried in his pewter and the Yokel contented himself with making his slice of black bread serve as trencher for his mess of meat, and consuming it as part of the meal.

Naturally the carving of the meat, fowl, or fish so that suitable portions could be served was a most important act, essential to the progress of the meal and the comfort of the family or guest. Robert May, in his book "The Accomplished Cook," which he published in 1667, gives these terms of carving, which are preceded by the invitation:

"Here's all the Forms of every Implement
"To work or carve with; so he makes thee able
"To deck the Dresser, and adorn the Table.
"And so you're welcome, pray fall to, and eat."

Terms of Carving

"Break that deer, leach that brawn, rear that goose, lift
"that swan, sauce that capon, spoil that hen, fruft that
"chicken, unbrace that mallard, unlace that coney, dismem-
"ber that hern, display that crane, disfigure that peacock,
"unjoint that bittern, untach that curlew, allay that pheasant,
"wing that partridge, wing that quail, mince that plover,
"thigh that pidgeon, border that pasty, thigh that woodcock,
"thigh all manner of small birds.

"Timber the fire, tire that egg, chine that salmon, string
"that lamprey, splat that pike, sauce that plaice, sauce that
"tench, splay that bream, side that haddock, tusk that barbel,
"culpon that trout, fin that chevin, transon that eel, tranch
"that sturgeon, undertranch that porpus, tame that crab,
"barb that lobster."

At banquets or suppers where desserts were most
elaborate, .diagrams or explicit details were provided for the butler and other officers, sometimes
called "serjeants and yeomen of the pantry."

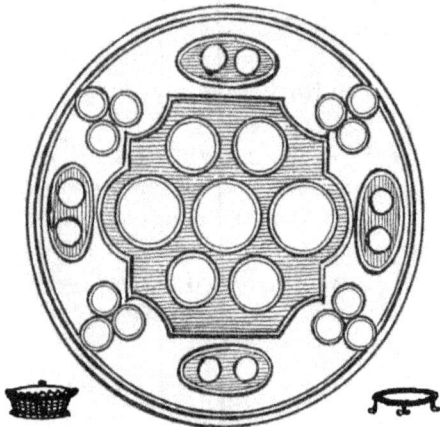

*Explication of a Banquet of Sweetmeats,
for a round table*

The banquet of sweetmeats or kickshaws were
disposed on silver dishes upon a central revolving
"machine" or top made of wood of osier or willow
for lightness. The elaborateness and splendor of
this arrangement was topped off with the Épergne,
on which large pyramids of fruit were placed care-

Banquet of Sweetmeats
Early seventeenth century

fully, composed of peaches, apples, plums, grapes,
and oranges, the latter the especial delight of Oliver
Cromwell, whose wife, Joan, rebukes him for his
excessive fondness, as unseemly and extravagant.

The whole was topped off with a glorious pineapple, frequently rented for the occasion, so the
stories go, and when a portion of pineapple was desired the tactful butler said, "The flavor of the
peaches is choice," and a portion of peaches was
served, so the pineapple passed intact to its next table.

The Nef

ONE of the most interesting of the ornaments of the table of that period was the Nef, of shiplike structure, usually of silver, sometimes of pewter, which served to contain the salt cellar, towel, or napkin of its lordly owner. It was usually topped off with his emblem,—in the illustration a bird is shown,—and it also carried the coat of arms.

The benches provided seating for the many; chairs were for the great people, so to sit on a chair was an event. Frequently the benches were boards on small trestles; when not in use they were folded and stored in corners of the great hall.

So lived the people of Merrie England five or more centuries ago, so they live to-day in other lands, and we may safely assume that the rise in the scale of socialized living is definitely marked by its table-setting standards.

The Nef
The urn for storing towel,
knife, and spoon for
table use

The lady of yesterday had to fulfil certain definite requirements; there was little guesswork concerning her tasks. These things were required of her. She must have skill in:

Household medication
Cereals—their condition
Cookery—its execution
Textiles—their dressing—Hemp—Flax—Wool
Spinning—the processes

Weaving—the manipulation and choice of looms
Dairy work—butter, cheese, etc.
Distillation—wines and simples
Baking—care of bake-house
Brewing—care of brew-house
Perfumes—their preparation
Sewing and fabrication of clothing
Dyeing—a knowledge of dye-stuffs

There is practically little mention of laundry and its work, for the simple reason that there was little body linen or clothes to launder, lingerie and night-dresses coming into use many years after the period. When the silken, velvet, or woolen gowns were soiled, they were put into the dye-pot.

An interesting story of the laying of Queen Elizabeth's table is Englished by Horace Walpole from an old letter of a traveler of that period as follows:

"A gentleman entered the room bearing a rod, and along "with him another who had a table-cloth, which, after they "both had kneeled three times with the utmost veneration, "he spread upon the table, and, after kneeling again, they "both retired.

"Then came two others, one with rod again, the other a "salt cellar, a plate, and bread; when they had kneeled as the "others had done and placed what was brought upon the "table, they too retired, with the same ceremonies performed "by the first.

"At last came an unmarried lady (said to be a Countess), "and along with her came a married one bearing a *tasting-* "*knife;* the former was dressed in white silk, so when she "had prostrated herself three times in a most graceful man- "ner, approached the table and rubbed the plates with bread "and salt, with as much care as if the Queen had been pres- "ent; when they had waited there a little time, the Yeomen "of the Guard entered, bareheaded, clothed in scarlet with a

"golden rose upon their backs, bringing in at each turn a
"course of 24 dishes served in plate; these dishes were re-

A Nice Party
A picnic dinner on the grass, in the fifteenth century.
Note plate for fowl and fish and the harpist to supply music .

"ceived by a gentleman in the same order they were brought
"and placed upon the table, while the lady taster gave to
"each guard a mouthful to eat, for fear of poison.

"During the time that this guard, which consisted of the
"tallest and stoutest men that could be found in all England,
"being carefully selected for this service, were bringing din-
"ner, 12 trumpets and 2 kettledrums made the hall ring for
"half an hour together.

"At the end of all this ceremonial, a number of unmarried
"ladies appeared, who with particular solemnity lifted the
"meat off the table and conveyed it into the Queen's inner
"and more private chamber, when, after she had chosen for
"herself, the rest goes to the ladies of the Court.

"The Queen sups and dines alone with very few attend-
"ants, and it is very seldom that anybody, foreigner or native,
"is admitted at that time, and then only at the intercession
"of somebody in power."

> From Paul Hentzner's *"Journey into England."*
> Printed at Strawberry Hill by
> Horace Walpole, 1717–1797.

The Silversmith's Shop and Tools
In the time of Edward III. Woman and servant purchasing
ewer and basin

The story of the entry on the stage of domestic
life of the various implements of tableware is a record of the advance in gentler living. Table manners
became a matter of convention as well as of fact,

showing definite progress in fastidious habits at the table.

In "Lady Rich's Closet" (1633), discussing the paper frill around the bony end of the leg of mutton which had already made its appearance, the lady was admonished to adopt the convenient instrument at the risk of being called over-dainty; in carving she was told "to distribute the best pieces first, and that it is decent to use a fork."

It was at about this period that women began to officiate at the head of the table in the useful task of carvers and distributors of the meat, which was passed out on a broad, flat knife, sometimes as much as four inches in width. Though this new duty brought with it the honor of promotion to a high place above the salt, they were really repeating their old task as distributors of the bread, as in earlier days.

The blue glass-lined Sugar Basket of Adam design; most popular in Colonial days

Careful instruction in carving and serving meats was given by teachers and professors in the gentle art of etiquette.

Among the points of behavior to be observed at the table were these: "To sit straight at table. Nor by ravenous gesture discover a voracious appetite. Talk not when you have meat in your mouth, nor venture to eat spoon-meat so hot as to bring tears to your eyes, which is unseemly."

The "hall-mark" of the graces of yesterday is found in the silver which has come down to the fortunate ones of to-day. Possible it is that this evidence of their genial living, happy thinking, is but the tangible heritage of the days gone by, and by the same evidence shall we be judged by our descendants, shall we leave them pewter, brass, or the honored and honorable silver, the queen of table metals.

There was something more in the development of table service than convenience or utility, for in this process came handsomer living and nicer and finer service. No longer did we feed as ravening wolves or hungry animals, but rather as humans of greater refinement.

The literature of the seventeenth century is redolent of good living and choice service. Samuel Pepys, our much loved diarist of that period, tells of his dinings, at which "We were merry," when careful cooking and fine living were more than a theory, rather an outward evidence of an inward desire for a more satisfactory rendering of culinary art.

Celtic Cup
Serpent handle

Silver has served a very definite use in this portrayal of home life and manners of the robust ages that precede us, for silver definitely marked the advance in riches of the individual as well as of the nation, and in the seventeenth century they certainly set great store or value on silver. Remember Pepys' disappointment at the christening when he "had provided six spoons and some plate against the child being named for him, and the Minister in christening pronounced the child's name John," and Samuel Pepys carried his silver spoons and plate home again.

Back in the sixteenth century we read that

Henry VII paid £1, 6 shillings, 8 pence for carving knives, and that Mistress Brent, in 1500, received 12 shillings for a silver fork weighing 3 ounces, a matter of very careful record.

Boiled and fried meats came to the table on silver, and the roasts on spits as they were lifted from the fire. Vegetables were also dressed in silver dishes, and as time progressed more and more articles of table service were fashioned from silver.

Social life was progressing merrily. In the sixteenth century, husband and wife ate from the same dish, as evidence of their faithfulness and love. Possibly the loving-cup is also a relic of that day. Men and women alternated at table, and the social

Salt Shaker
Colonial model

graces developed and the amenities of life increased. With the handsomer service came courtesy and kindliness. Table manners, tablesetting, and table equipment progressed rapidly from the reign of Henry VIII, who started the movement for more luxurious living, to the period in which his daughter Elizabeth held sway. So symbolic was it that Shakespeare makes one of his women characters reproach her husband with the fact that she had not dipped fingers in the dish with him for many months.

Then came the picture of Queen Elizabeth conferring the degree of knighthood on the loin of beef, the ceremony of which is described in "The Knighting of Sir-Loin."

Silver Compote

The Knighting of Sir-Loin

ELIZABETH TUDOR her breakfast would make
On a pot of strong beer and a pound of beefsteak
Ere six in the morning was toll'd by the chimes—
Oh, the days of Queen Bess, they were merry old times!

From hawking and hunting she rode back to town,
In time just to knock an ambassador down;
Toy'd, trifled, coquetted, then lopped off a head;
And at threescore and ten danced a hornpipe to bed.

With Nicholas Bacon, her councillor chief,
One day she was dining on English roast beef;
That very same day when her Majesty's Grace
Had given Lord Essex a slap in the face.

My Lord Keeper stared, as the wine-cup she kissed,
At his sovereign lady's superlative twist.
And thought, thinking truly, his larder would squeak,
He'd much rather keep her a day than a week.

"What call you this dainty, my very good Lord?"
"The Loin," bowing low till his nose touched the board.
"And, breath of our nostrils and light of our eyes,
Saving your presence, the ox was a prize!"

"Unsheathe me, mine host, thy Toledo so bright,
Delicious Sir-Loin, I do dub thee a knight!
Be thine at our banquets of honor the post;
While the Queen rules the realm, let Sir-Loin rule the
    roast."

                    —Anonymous.

Spoons were *the* table utensil. They were not provided by the host, but each guest produced from his pocket his own spoon to use during his visit, were that for a meal or a month.

These spoons, usually of elaborate design, were often gifts of one of the sponsors at baptism. Chief among favorite designs for these spoons was the well known Apostle spoon. A rich child with wealthy godparents would probably receive all twelve of the Apostles; the more humble, one or two.

Poor folks must carry their own spoons as well as the rich, but theirs were usually of tinned iron and were called "Latten spoons." It is easily seen how our still existing saying, "Born with a silver spoon in his mouth," originated. It meant more than wealth, for possessors of a silver spoon sat, d u r i n g the medieval times, at the table on the dais; later they sat above the dividing line of the general table—always marked by the elaborate standard of all, high above the salt. Lower down came those who were endowed only with the "Latten spoon"; and least of all, very far from the honor-conferring salt, were placed those who were armed with spoons of wood.

The Apostle Spoon

with Dove in center; sixteenth century, one of a set of twelve representing the Apostolic group

Florentine Table-spoon

Rich ornamentation design, showing Italian influence

Forks

FORKS came later, and their introduction produced much criticism, the objectors holding that
"fingers were made before forks" was not to be
gainsaid, but, as usual, progress marched forward
with precision and decision.

Forks came from Italy, and
Thomas Coryat's letters of 1608
cites the new discovery as almost
as important as the discovery of
America, and causing far more dis-
cussion. Coryat writes: "The Ital-
ians, as well as strangers in Italy,
do always at their meals use a little
fork when they cut their meat."

It was bad form to put the
fingers to the meat dish, and worse
manners, which gave offense to all
the company, to carry the meat
from the plate or dish with the
fingers.

The forks were of iron or steel,
and some silver ones, these being
used only by gentlemen.

"Queen Elizabeth had at least
three forks: one of crystal garnished with gold and sparks of
garnets; another of coral slightly
garnished with gold; and a third
of gold, garnished with two little
rubies, two little pearls pendant, and a coral." But
they could only have been meant as curios; they were
not meant for eating the Michaelmas goose, of
which she was so fond.

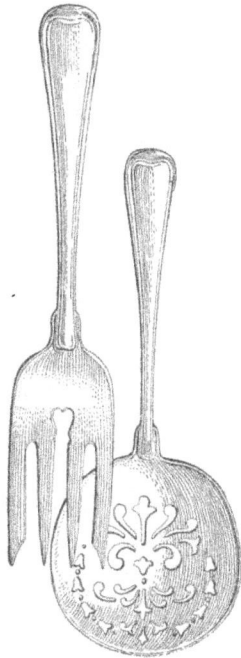

*Old French Cold Meat
Fork and Tomato Server*

To Coryat belongs the honor of first laying the
forks on the table, and though the pulpit denounced
and the public raged, forks had come to stay.

Florentine Plate
Of rich design, showing Medici influence

In 1652 Heylin alludes to the use of silver forks,
and in the days of Charles II forks were in common
use.

They were usually of steel, sometimes of two
prongs, occasionally of six; the handles were of many
materials and scores of shapes; some had green,
some pink, and some yellow handles, but the silver
fork was rare till the beginning of the nineteenth
century.

The fork did much for the simplification and ad-
vancement of culinary art by encouraging the taste

for solid viands and natural flavors. The use of the fork made possible the delicate slice as against the gobbets of meat of the century before, and, also, the fork promoted cleanliness at the table in contrast with the messy days when fingers were used in the bowls.

The introduction of the fork also made possible choicer table linen, finer cloths, and handsome napkins.

There soon developed definite rules for folding and laying the napkin, so that there was published diagrams showing twenty-five ways to fold a napkin.

Knives, forks and spoons, platters, ewers and basins being introduced and accounted for, the custom of a more dignified setting of table became

Potato Ring
About eight inches in diameter, in which whole potatoes were
served. The ring was set either on china or silver
plate. Early eighteenth century

popular. With the improvement of table appliances, manners improved and culinary art advanced to higher standards, the better to fit the richer and more elaborate tablesetting and silver service.

The program of the social amenities began to develop in the time of Queen Anne, who was an adept in culinary art and a devotee of gastronomic delights.

The men and women of that period were good stout trencher-folk, and life was expressed in good eating.

In this period a more attractive and more stately service for meals was developed. Silversmiths were set at work to achieve higher standards of art in metal-work, and royalty gave the sign for higher standards of living and more delicate methods of eating.

Coffee-pot
Queen Anne period.
Sets well on the table

Before forks came into use it was the duty of the carver who stood near the table to cut the slices of meat in a gobbet, then slit the slice in four almost to the top, so that it could more daintily be bitten and more conveniently masticated.

Coryat in his interesting letters from Italy describes the use of forks. He writes:

"For while with their knife which they hold in one hand
"they cut the meat out of the dish, they fasten their fork,
"which they hold in their other hand upon the same dish, so
"that whatsoever he be that sitting in the company of any
"others at meal, should unadvisedly touch the dish of meat
"with his fingers, from which all at the table do cut, he will
"give occasion of offence unto the company, as having trans-
"gressed the laws of good manners, in so much that for his
"error he shall be at the least brow-beaten, if not repre-
"hended in words. Hereupon I myself thought good to imi-
"tate the Italian fashion not only when I was in Italy but in-
"England since I came home."

Large platters appeared for holding the generous roasts and the gaily ornamented fowl and the service of fish was highly decorated.

Queen Anne, with her friend Sarah Jennings, first Duchess of Marlborough, did much to develop the amenities of dining; it was a gay age, for wealth was increasing rapidly from the American colonies, as well as from other sources. Table silver, then as now, was the evidence of its presence and the expression of the good taste and fine judgment of the possessor. The choicest heirlooms of to-day are the fine tableware of silver of that and succeeding periods, and from that period date our present standards of good living and its culinary art.

Muffineer
From which soft sugar
was shaken over fruits
and cakes at table.
William and Mary period

The succeeding Georgian period, including George I, II, III, and IV, gave much in dignified table service to the present time, and examples of it are much sought for.

The scene of silver-making activities now shifts from the Merrie England of the four Georges to the bleak American shores, for here was made, even in the earliest days, silver tableware of excellent design and correct form.

Many of our pieces of early Colonial design and

fabrication have been unjustly credited to British origin and English design, on the presumption that their high quality of craftsmanship could not have been produced in America at that early date.

Silversmithing is an early American art. There was a silversmith named Thomas Howard, registered in Jamestown, Virginia, in the 1620 arrivals, and in 1634 John Mansfield was a silversmith working in Charlestown, Massachusetts.

Jacobean Vegetable Dish
Richly ornate

In the period from 1650 to 1730, some excellent work was produced and silver spoons with trifid handles—monograms on back—are still in existence.

There were domed and globular tea-pots, or fat and thin, as they were frequently described. There were, of course, tankards, beakers, and cups, and always very good salt cellars, the salt cellar still holding its favored place on the table.

Also there were interesting and now obsolete pieces—the Potato Ring and the Muffineer. The Potato Ring was a ring of pierced and wrought silver, large enough to encircle a moderate-sized platter and hold in place a good mound of baked or boiled potatoes. The Muffineer may be called the progenitor of our salt shakers, except that it was intended for sugar and not salt.

From 1730 to 1765, the designs for spoons were

more varied, the most common design being the one
described as "rat tail." With the advent of Paul
Revere into the art of silversmithing came a broad-
ening of design, for the Revere designs include
scroll embellishments such as cockle-shells, sometimes birds; the front of the handle was decorated,
and a more artistic effect secured. More kinds of

A most dignified rendering of Georgian period.
Adam design

spoons were made, such as salt spoons and marrow
spoons with their usual bowl and the handle drawn
into a long narrow scoop.

The first forks made here were done by John
Noyes of Boston, 1674–1749, and are now in the
Boston Museum. They have silver handles and
steel prongs.

Knives were occasionally made with silver handles, but they were rare, most of them having bone
grasps. So much for early flatware.

A Wedgwood Design Tea-pot

Porringers of silver were in early use and bear
the somewhat earliest dates of all hollow tableware.
Tea-pots, coffee-pots, cups, tureens, sugar-bowls, and
platters, as well as silver patch boxes to carry the
ever-present piecework of the day, followed, as the
wealth of the colonies increased and their living grew
more comfortable. Silver expressed best the choicer
family pride and gave evidence of richer family traditions.

The Gorham Mark

While New York, Philadelphia, Baltimore, and
other places produced choice silver and other wares,
the center of the industry has always been in New
England. In the lists of the early silversmiths we
find Jabez Gorham recorded as a silversmith in

Providence, Rhode Island, in 1792, and in 1820 John Gorham was entered as a silversmith.

Then, in New Haven, Connecticut, Miles Gorham antedated both, for he is of definite record as a silversmith, with the dates of 1757–1847, a period of ninety years.

Small wonder that our best traditions of silver lie with the house of the Gorham associates, who so splendidly carry forward the traditions and examples of the earliest members of the house.

Tea-caddy
Probably of the period of Restoration.
Early seventeenth century

The Well-Dressed Table

LINENS FOR BREAKFAST, LUNCHEON, *and* DINNER

THE two informal meals of breakfast and luncheon give scope for variety in tablesetting and use of color in the linen. Over the bare table oblong mats and runners of crash or linen, white or colored, may be effectively used, with small napkins to match.

The luncheon table will be a trifle more elaborate than that of breakfast. The mats and runners will

A Delightful Silver Dinner Service
Of Plymouth pattern, with Cleremont flatware in position

be white instead of colored, and the napkins with
them of the conventional luncheon size, that is, four-
teen to seventeen inches square.

If a formal luncheon is served, a lace or em-
broidery-trimmed cloth which follows the shape of
the table is often used. Napkins of the conventional
luncheon size will, in this case, be decorated to match
the cloth used. Exquisite
cloths of this description
can be obtained.

At dinner, the heavy
damask cloth is pre-
ferred. It is usually un-
adorned save for the pat-
tern in the linen itself or
by one handsome mono-
gram. The dinner cloth,
to be quite correct, should
always be rectangular,

Richly Decorated Sauce-boat
Showing Greek influence in design

never round, no matter what the shape of the table.
Dinner napkins are also of heavy damask, twenty-
six to thirty-six inches square.

Whenever a table-cloth is used, it should be laid
over a silence cloth of white, thick, double-faced
material. This silence cloth should extend five inches
over each side of the table.

Linens may be omitted entirely, if desired. There
is nothing more beautiful and correct than a silver
service laid directly on the bare surface of beautifully
polished wood.

Laying the Table

FIRST of all the table should be adjusted so that
each person to be served will have at least
twenty-five inches space for service.

If the table is being set for breakfast or an informal luncheon, the mats or runners are carefully arranged on the bare table, or, if desired, a low centerpiece on a center mat is arranged. Good taste demands something very simple, a bowl of flowers or fruit, and should by all means be low enough so as in no way to cut off one side of the table from the other, thus impeding general conversation.

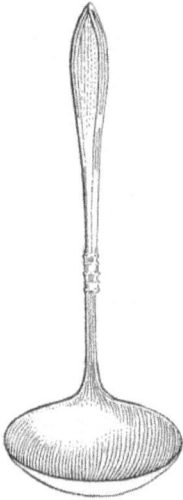

In preparing the table for dinner, the silence cloth should first be laid, then the table-cloth, straight and smooth, with lengthwise fold in the exact center. Mathematical precision is the rule in regard to the laying of silver. It should be laid one half inch in from the edge of the table, very compactly and neatly, knives with cutting edges toward the plate, and spoons in general being laid to the right of the cover, forks on the left, arranged in the order in which they are to be used, the one first to be used being farthest from the plate.

One exception to the general rule occurs when oysters are the first course to be served at a luncheon or dinner. If the oyster-fork is supplied with the rest of the silver at the

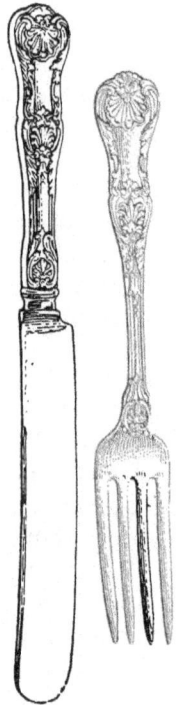

Colonial
Portsmouth Ladle
Graceful in line
and simple in
decoration

King Pattern of
Flatware
One of the earliest
Colonial designs,
still in use by the
older families

cover, it may take its place at the extreme right of the cover, just before the spoons and knives.

The matter of supplying silver for all the courses when the cover is laid is optional. It may be brought in with the courses as they are served, if preferred.

In the absence of a waitress, it saves confusion to have the silver all laid and ready.

Attractive Decoration for Table
Showing Silver Compotes and Vases—all hand-made
French—Martelé design

The napkin, neatly folded, is placed to the right of the cover, one half inch from the edge of the table, with hemmed edge uppermost; and if folded squarely, the hemmed edge should be parallel to both the edges of the table and to the cover.

Glasses are placed just above the knives and slightly to the right. Just before the meal is announced, they should be filled three quarters full. Bread and butter are not usually served at the formal dinner, but are often desired for the informal or family dinner. When they are to be served, bread and butter plates are placed at the upper left-hand side of the cover, at the tip of the forks. Butter spreaders are laid across the bread and butter plates. Butter is supplied on each bread and butter plate just before the meal is announced.

A Chippendale Coffee-urn

Salt and pepper may be supplied individually, in which case they occupy a place just in front of each cover; or they may be placed between each two covers, or nearing the corners of the table, just on a line with the top edge of the plate.

Chairs should be placed at each cover, but should not touch the table itself.

General Service

THE meal should be announced quietly, either by the waitress, a daughter of the family who will act in the capacity of waitress, or by the hostess herself.

In case a waitress or daughter of the family makes the announcement, she speaks only to the hostess, who in turn indicates to the guests that all is in readiness.

For informal family service, when there is no waitress, a member of the family may quietly leave the table when it is time to attend to details of removing a course and bringing on a new one, or supplying water, butter, and so forth. The tea-wagon may be used informally by the hostess for such meals as breakfast and luncheon. It may stand at her right, and may have upon it the dishes for the courses which follow.

In this case the hostess removes to the tea-wagon all the large dishes or platters of food. These will be followed by the used plates and silver, and the table being thus cleared of one course, the guests will be served from the tea-wagon with plates and silver required for the next.

If thought is expended on this type of service, it may be accomplished very smoothly and efficiently, and no one will have to leave the table. How-ever, everything must be in readiness before the meal begins and no detail forgotten.

French Soup and Bouillon Spoons
Ancient model

When service is to be given by a waitress or some member of the family, there are a few simple rules to remember.

Everything except beverages should be served and removed from the left of a guest. In offering a dish of food be sure its spoon and fork are convenient to

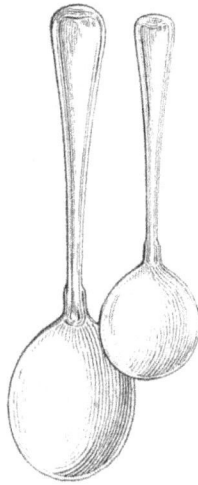

the person being served, and offer such dishes at the left of a guest and when removing plates, etc. *Never reach across a cover.*

Beverages are served from the right. Glasses, cups, and saucers are removed from the right.

Serve the hostess, then the guest of honor, who will be seated at the right of the hostess, then the guest next at the right of the host, and so on until all are served. The host is usually served last.

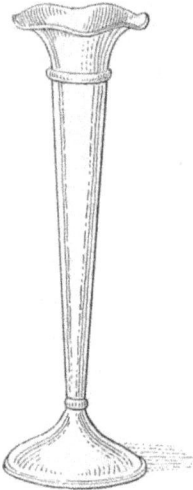

When changing a course, everything that will not be required by a later course should be removed. Large dishes containing food should be removed first, then soiled silver, china, and glass. If there is any unused silver, china, or glassware, remove it next and follow this, if necessary, by removing crumbs from the table with a small plate and a clean, folded napkin.

When the waitress, in informal service, wishes to remove a course as quickly as possible, she may take one dish with her left hand, transfer it to her right, and remove another with her left, thus going away with both hands full, and, if possible, leaving the cover entirely cleared, a highly desirable result.

A dignified and attractive Silver Vase of early Colonial period

As soon as one course has been entirely removed, the waitress should place the silver for the next course, if it has not previously been placed at each cover. After she has supplied each guest with the following course, she should not resume her seat or retire until she has filled the water glasses and, if necessary, supplied bread and butter.

A plate containing bread and one containing butter-balls (with butter fork), as well as a carafe containing water, should be upon the serving table for the convenience of the waitress.

After-Theatre Supper Service
Rarebit and tasty bite in readiness

Late Supper

THE crowning touch to the theater party or the returning guests from the dinner dance is a tasty bit of supper which enhances the lingering memory of the evening's entertainment.

At this feast no servant enters; the chafing-dish serves as stove, the host or hostess serves as chef, the fortunate guests as servers, and mirth presides, be the menu a simple rarebit or a more complex chicken à la King. The tablesetting is simple, as outlined, and then—"let joy be unconfined."

The chafing-dish, set at a convenient place, is the focal center of the snack, for such it is to the fortunate guest. The bread, thinly sliced and folded in a napkin, adjoins the electric toaster; the silver dish for the tasty rarebit shines with luster of true silver.

The Service of Fruits

LITTLE details of serving food are, after all, the things which "make or mar" an otherwise perfect meal. Even breakfast can be so daintily and deftly served that to partake of it becomes a real event and source of satisfaction.

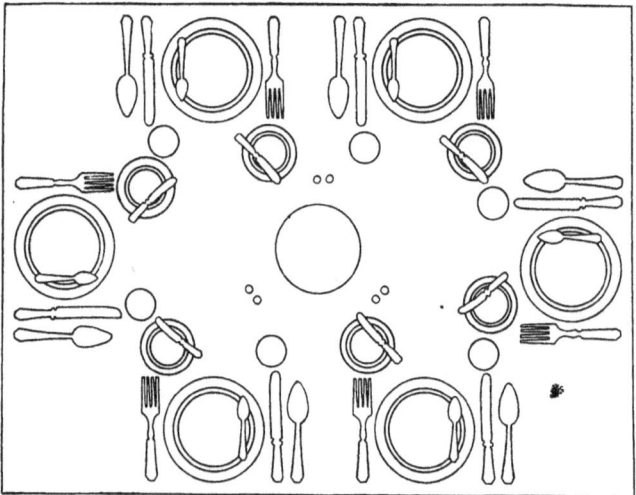

Setting of Breakfast Table

What are the correct methods of serving fruits? An apple should either be served on a plate about six inches in diameter and accompanied by a silver

fruit-knife so that the guest may cut it into quarters
and peel it at his pleasure, or the fruit plate and

A Breakfast Service of Plymouth Design Flatware
Cleremont pattern

knife may be brought to the table first and laid in
front of the guest, and then a fruit dish with apples
may be passed by the waitress.

Other fruits served in the same
way as apples are pears, plums,
apricots, and mandarins.

Fresh berries, strawberries, black-
berries, blueberries, raspberries, as
well as currants, baked apples,
stewed prunes, stewed peaches, apricots, and all cooked fruits are served
in sauce dishes which rest upon small
service plates, and should be accompanied by a fruit-spoon, unless the
table has been laid with all the silver
which will be needed. With all
soft fruit served in this.way, the

Marmalade Jar
Colonial glass
Marmalade Spoon
ready for service of
breakfast or tea

waitress should pass fine granulated or powdered
sugar and cream. When there is no waitress, these
may be passed at the table.

Strawberries, when very large, are sometimes

served with the stems left on, in which case they should be on plates of the same size as those used for apples, and should be accompanied by a spoonful of powdered sugar on the side of the plate.

Fruit Bowl
Early Colonial design, an heirloom
of Colonial days

Peaches may be served whole in the same way as apples, or they may be peeled and sliced and served as berries or other soft fruits are served.

Nectarines, a variety of peach with soft skin, may be served in the same way as peaches. They are usually served whole.

To serve grapes, each person is supplied by the waitress with a fruit plate; then a compote containing the grapes, accompanied by grape-shears, is passed by the waitress, who cuts the bunches for each person, as desired. Grapes may also be served individually in clear glass bowls with iced water.

Cherries are served from a compote in the same way as grapes, each guest having been supplied with fruit plate and finger-bowl.

One half of a large grape-fruit is usually served to one person. It is carefully prepared with tough center removed, and may have had sugar previously added, if desired. It should come on a fruit plate, or in a special grape-fruit bowl, with small service plate underneath, accompanied by an orange-spoon. The waitress should see that more sugar is supplied to those desiring it.

One type of old
Salt Cellar

Oranges may be served in a variety of ways. They may be served from the compote, each guest having a fruit plate, fruit-knife, and fruit-spoon. In this case sugar should be passed by the waitress, as soon as the guests have cut their oranges and are ready. A very usual way of serving this fruit is to cut it in half and serve on fruit plate with orange-spoon. In this case the waitress passes the sugar to each person.

If a sliced orange be served (having been peeled also) on a fruit plate, then it may be eaten with a fork, but if served whole or halved in a dish such as used for berries, an orange spoon is used.

A Colonial Salt Cellar of charming design

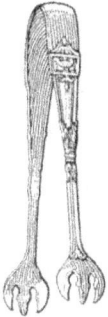

Sugar Tongs of Lansdown pattern

Cantaloupe, filled with cracked ice, is served in halves or quarters on fruit plates (or in a special fruit dish, such as is sometimes used for grape-fruit), and should be accompanied by a fruit-spoon. Sugar, salt, and pepper are supplied by the waitress.

Honeydew melon is served in the same way as cantaloupe, and is usually accompanied by a slice of lemon.

Watermelon is cut in wedges or circles, and is served on a fruit plate larger than the usual fruit plate, and a fruit-knife as well as fork may be provided.

The finger-bowl plays an important part in the serving of most fruits. Indeed, it is indispensable except when berries or sliced fruits are served.

In the absence of a waitress, fruit may be served individually at each cover before the members of the family and guests are seated.

The Service of Cereals

"HOT things hot" is a good rule to remember when serving cooked cereals, such as rolled oats, cracked wheat, corn-meal mush, and hominy grits. These may come from the kitchen served in individual bowls on service plates and accompanied by a spoon, unless sufficient silver for all the courses has previously been laid at each cover. The waitress offers sugar and cream to each person, or these may be passed at the table in the absence of a waitress. Many persons prefer brown sugar served with these cooked cereals.

Cereals may also be served by the host from a porringer, a large serving spoon being used. Individual cereal bowls are brought to him, and as he serves each of these the waitress carries it to the guest. If there is no waitress, these may be passed from the head of the table as each bowl is served.

Etruscan Fork Including the Greek motif in design

Ready-cooked, dried cereals are served in the same way, following in addition any special directions which may be on the box containing the cereal. The invariable rule should be to reheat but not brown the ready-to-eat flakes or the puffed grains. This treatment will give them the desirable crispness which always enhances the flavor.

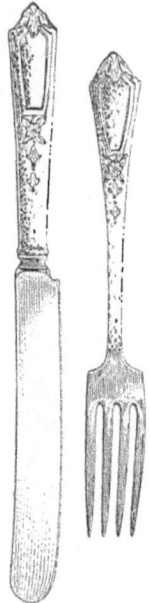

A modern design showing hammered effect, commonly called Pattern A

The Service of Toast and Hot Cakes

TOAST, as needed, is best made at the table with
an electric toaster. If toast, French toast, hot
cakes, or waffles are brought from the kitchen, have
the plate containing them covered with a perforated
silver cover. Do not cover it with a soup plate or
bowl. This makes toast soggy. The very convenient and attractive toast rack or a silver bread
tray is frequently used for dry toast. When waffles,
hot cakes, or French toast are served, the syrup
should not be forgotten. Also a dish containing a mixture of pulverized sugar and
cinnamon might be provided, as some
prefer this to the syrup.

Service of Eggs

Cooked in Shell, Coddled, or Boiled

SERVE medium and soft-cooked eggs
either in egg-cup or egg-glass with six-
inch plate under cup or glass. Eggs served
in this way may come directly from the
kitchen as individual service. Each one
should be accompanied by silver egg cut-
ter, and also by a spoon, unless sufficient
silver has been laid at the cover.

*Tea and Table-
Spoons
Cleremont pat-
tern, typical
Colonial design*

Hard-boiled eggs may be served in
vegetable dishes or on small plates. If the
vegetable dish is used, it should have a six-
inch plate under it.

Each person being served should already have
been supplied with large service plate, so that the
six-inch plate containing the egg-cup or other dish
may be set at the upper left of each cover.

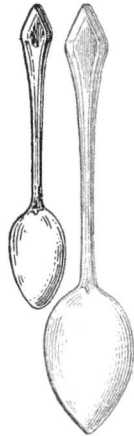

Eggs

Eggs Poached on Toast

A SMALL platter containing individual portion is set just above each service plate. Serving spoon should be provided.

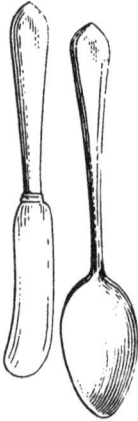

Shirred Eggs

SERVE in individual shirred egg dishes, set upon small plates and set to the left of each cover. The guest should previously have been supplied with the service plate.

Scrambled Eggs

SERVE individual portion on small platter just above each service plate and supply spoon to each guest; or serve on larger platter, placing before host. In this case have all the service plates also before the host, or the waitress may bring them to him one or two at a time. Large spoon for serving will be required. Waitress may pass individual portions as served, or they may be passed at the table from guest to guest.

Old London Teaspoon and Butter Spread

Omelet

SERVE large-sized omelet on large platter, have all service plates hot when placed before the host; or the waitress may bring him one or two at a time. A serving spoon and serving fork to be used in separating the portions of the omelet will be required. The waitress may pass the individual portions as they are served, or, as is customary with scrambled eggs, they may be passed at the table from host to guest.

The Rasher of Bacon

TO the American trained in the food lore of the Anglo-Saxons a breakfast without its rasher of bacon ushers in a day foredoomed to disappointments. The crisp curled slices, browned to a delectable hue, served on the hot shining silver platter, will change the most taciturn to a happy smiling vis-à-vis.

Bread Tray, Cooked Cereal Dish, and Portsmouth Candlesticks

The Loaf Giver

THE revival of the use of the decorated bread-board with its silver bread-knife with which the thin slices are cut and placed on the electric toaster is a return to the charming personal service when the lady was in truth the Loaf Giver, the dispenser of the "staff of life" to all who came to her castle door.

It means the adapting of the present lack of home service so that the resulting good makes for the fine courtesy of personal service—the give and take between equals.

Child's Service

AT THOSE meals at which either the children of the household or visitors' children appear at table, it is well to provide for them the regular child's service.

Attractive little knives and forks, as well as spoons and "pushers," are now made especially for the use of these small folk.

The Baby's Silver Service
The pride of the home. Hammered so as not to show mar

It is wise also to have at the child's place a tray which is so designed as to fit along the edge of the table, and of sufficient size to hold most of the things used during the meal.

The value of correct table service for children cannot be overestimated, for not only does the child enjoy having his own porringer, mug, and small pitcher containing his milk, as well as the small size flat silver, but having the proper "utensils" and "tools" aid in teaching him to be independent and neat at table.

Unless a fresh napkin be provided for each meal, a small silver marker bearing the child's own monogram should be provided for his napkin, and the clasps for holding the napkin in place during the meal should accompany it.

Details of Luncheon and
Dinner Service

Service of Fruit Cocktails

THESE are served in cocktail glasses set upon
small plates, and a spoon should either accompany each, laid on the plate at the side of the cocktail glass, or should have been placed at the extreme
right of the cover when the table was laid.

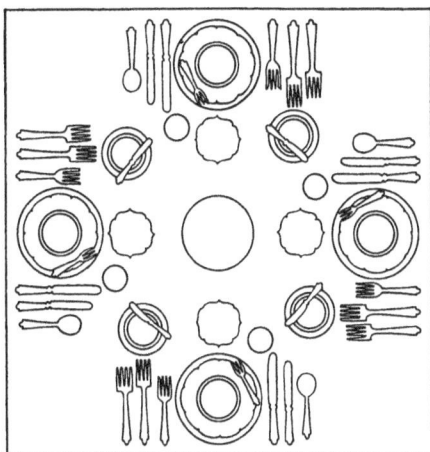

Setting of Luncheon Table

Just before the meal is announced, these may be
placed one at each cover, or they may be served after
the guests are seated.

Service of Oysters and Clams

OYSTERS or clams, as appetizers, are served in the half-shell on a bed of cracked ice, a deep plate being used for the purpose. This is usually set upon a somewhat larger plate in order to protect the

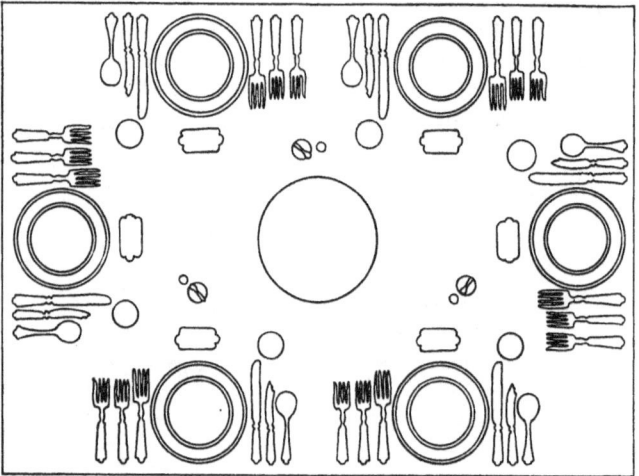

Setting of Dinner Table

table should the ice melt and overflow. They are accompanied by an oyster-fork, unless this has been laid previously at the extreme right of the cover. One fourth of a lemon should be laid in the center of each plate.

Sometimes, however, oysters appear as cocktails and are then dressed with sauce and served in a cocktail glass set upon a small plate, accompanied by an oyster-fork.

Oysters or clams on the half-shell may be placed

at each cover before the meal is announced, but it is
a little better to serve them just after the guests are
seated.

Service of Soups

SHOULD the meal begin with soup, the table
should be laid so that a large service plate is at
each cover, with soup spoons at the extreme right of
the cover. The napkin should be placed on the service plate, monogram uppermost. The dinner roll
may be slipped in its folds. When these have been
removed, the waitress places upon each service plate
a smaller, deeper plate containing soup. When the
soup is finished, the waitress removes both soup and
service plate.

Hand-wrought Fish Service
Martelé design

Service of Fish and Meat

PLATTERS of fish or meat can be so prepared
in the kitchen that the guests at table may serve
themselves from a dish passed by the waitress. This
is always true in service à la russe.

If desired, the host may carve the meat at the
table, the waitress standing beside him at his left,

ready to take each plate as it is filled, from the left
with her right hand, taking it to the guest, and returning to stand beside the carver.   All the plates
may be placed before the carver at once, or the
waitress may bring a fresh plate each time from the
side table.   When the number to be served is over
four the latter is better.

To add to the charm of the table,
handsome holder of the candle of the period
of Louis XV

In case some member of the family has acted as
waitress in bringing to the host the meat for service,
she may return to her place, and the plates, as filled,
may be passed from one to another by those seated
at the table.

Service of Vegetables

I T WILL usually be found best to have the waitress pass the vegetables to each guest, allowing him to help himself with large serving spoon and fork. She should offer such dishes from the left, placing the serving spoon and fork convenient to the guest and using a folded napkin beneath the

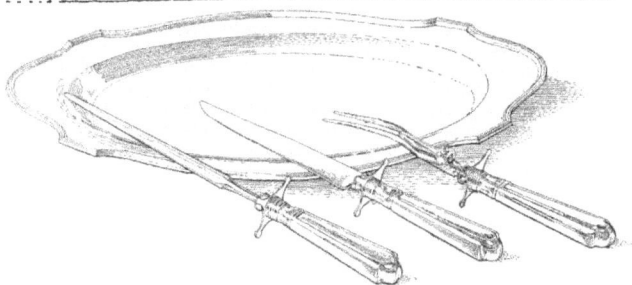

The dignity of the silver meat service. Platter of Plymouth design, the carvers silver handled, strong, yet graceful and sturdy

dish. The double service silver vegetable dish is excellent for vegetables served in this way.

In informal family service, where a member of the family has acted as waitress, these vegetables may be served by the host with the meat course, or another member of the family seated at his right may assist him by serving vegetables on the plate which he has supplied with meat.

Service of Salads

E VERYTHING used in making a salad should be cold and crisp. Even the plates on which it is to be served should be chilled. A warm salad is an abomination.

Individual salads should be served on eight-inch plates, and may be accompanied by wafers, crisp, buttered crackers, or sandwiches. Crackers, wafers, or sandwiches may be passed by the waitress after the salad is served. With the crackers or wafers, cream cheese may also be served. Bar-le-duc, guave jelly, or strawberry jam may be passed with salads that are dressed with French dressing.

If there is to be a salad, salad forks should be provided in laying the cover. Salad usually comes as a separate course after the meat and vegetables. At a luncheon it may be the main course.

If the salad is to be dressed at the table, the waitress places before the host the chilled individual salad plates, a bowl containing the ingredients chilled for the salad, silver stands containing salt, pepper, and paprika shakers, a peppercorn grinder, a bottle of Worcestershire sauce, a vinegar cruet, an olive oil cruet, and the mustard jar and silver spoon. The waitress should also provide the hostess with silver-handled, olive wood tined and bowled salad fork and spoon.

A separate bowl may be used for mixing the dressing. The oil is poured first and the seasonings added, then it is thinned with vinegar, which may be tarragon or estragon vinegar, as preferred. The epicure who is exacting in his taste will demand that the bowl be first rubbed with the cut surface of a clove of garlic, thus giving to the dressing the accent necessary to successful flavoring.

Fairfax Oyster Fork
A charming example of Virginia influence

Fairfax Salad Fork
A graceful adaptation of an early Colonial design

The dressing made in this way is then poured upon the salad and the whole tossed lightly for a few seconds before serving.

Another way of preparing the dressing is to hold the salad spoon over the bowl containing the ingredients for the salad, put into it the salt and pepper

The Service of Sheraton influence

and other seasonings, then fill the spoon with oil. Mix with a fork and pour upon the salad, distributing well. Then add the rest of the oil, a spoonful at a time, tossing the salad lightly after each addition. Lastly add the vinegar, toss again, and serve.

It is perfectly correct to serve the salad without dressing, thus giving to each guest the privilege of taking more or less of the dressing, as desired.

In this case either the French or the mayonnaise dressing is served in a silver bowl on its tray with the salad spoon beside it, the waitress serving to the left of the guest, who helps himself. In the absence of the waitress, the hostess passes the salad dressing to the guest of honor, who, after helping himself, passes it on to the next guest at his right.

Plymouth Salad Service of charming design

A Salad

To make this condiment, your poet begs
The pounded yellow of two hard-boiled eggs;
Two boiled potatoes, passed through kitchen-sieve
Smoothness and softness to the salad give;
Let onion atoms lurk within the bowl,
And, half-suspected, animate the whole.
Of mordant mustard add a single spoon,
Distrust the condiment that bites so soon;
But deem it not, thou man of herbs, a fault
To add a double quantity of salt.
And, lastly, o'er the flavored compound toss
A magic soup-spoon of anchovy sauce.
Oh, green and glorious! Oh, herbaceous treat!
'Twould tempt the dying anchorite to eat;
Back to the world he'd turn his fleeting soul,
And plunge his fingers in the salad bowl!
Serenely full, the epicure would say,
Fate cannot harm me, I have dined today!

—Sidney Smith.

Service of Bread and Butter

WHEN bread and butter are to be served, a bread and butter plate is provided, and takes its place at the upper left of the cover. Individual butter spreaders are placed on these plates. Just before the meal, pats of butter should be distributed, and the waitress replenishes these as the meal progresses.

Placing a dinner roll in the folds of the napkin, either upon the plate or when the napkin lies to one side of the plate, is a convenient method of supplying the guests with bread at the beginning of a meal, and the waitress or member of the family acting as such may pass rolls or other bread from time to time.

Service of Desserts

BEFORE the dessert is served, all the other dishes are removed from the table, and the waitress or member of the family acting in that capacity brushes the crumbs from the table, using a folded napkin and a plate.

Silver for dessert will probably have been laid with the cover when the table was set, but the silver to be used will depend largely on what the dessert is to be. For ice-cream, particularly the brick ice-cream, the ice-cream spoon with prongs should be used.

At formal luncheons and dinners it is good form as the salad service is removed to place before each guest a dainty or elaborate glass or silver finger-bowl and plate. Under the finger-bowl and on the plate rests a filmy linen or lace doily, which each guest removes with the finger-bowl, placing both to the left above the plate. Upon this plate the dessert may be served, or it may be removed as the dessert on its own plate is placed in front of the guest.

Later the finger-bowl is placed in front of the guest, or the guest himself removes it to a convenient place, where the tips of the fingers, which may have touched food, are gently dipped in the water and dried daintily on the napkin; a subtle reminder to the initiate that while we have advanced far, we still retain the form of bowl, laver, and towel of the pre-forkless age.

In less formal dinners the sweet dessert may be omitted and the cheese, hard crackers, or toasted wafers and coffee substituted.

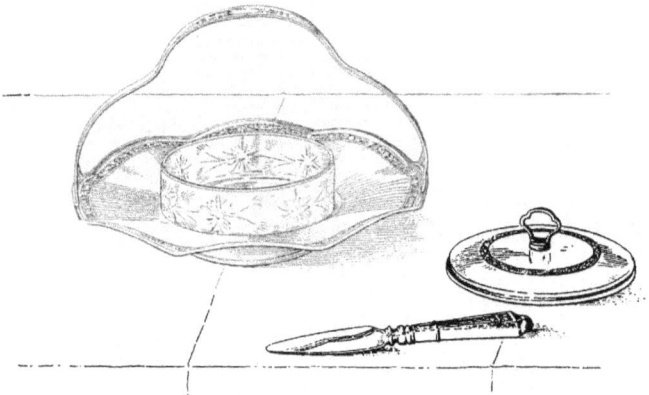

An Effective Cheese Service

Service of Cheese

CHEESE is often served at the end of a meal. American cheese, Vermont sage cheese, Waukesha cream cheese, Schweitzer cheese, and fromage de Brie are served on individual small plates with doilies and accompanied in each case by a cheese-knife and crackers.

Neufchâtel, Camembert, and Roquefort, as well as Sapsago cheese, are served, a small wedge to each person, on small plates with butter, and accompanied by a butter-knife.

Edam and pineapple cheese should be served from a large dish. Some of the cheese should be cut and accompanied by a cheese-knife and a plate of crackers. Each guest will help himself. It is also proper to serve Edam cheese from a cheese stand with a cheese-knife.

"Who Can Live Without Dining?"

WE may live without poetry, music and art;
We may live without conscience, and live without heart;
We may live without friends; we may live without books;
But civilized man cannot live without cooks.

We may live without books—what is knowledge but
    grieving?
We may live without hope—what is hope but deceiving?
We may live without love—what is passion but pining?
But where is the man who can live without dining?

                —*Owen Meredith.*

Coffee for Breakfast and Luncheon

COFFEE for breakfast or luncheon may be made on the table with an electric percolator, if desired, and, in any case, it may be poured by the hostess. The waitress will take each cup as it is filled to a guest. In the absence of a waitress, these may be passed at the table. When coffee is poured by the hostess at the table, she frequently adds cream and sugar also, after ascertaining the wishes of the guest for whom she is preparing the cup of coffee.

Ordinarily the teaspoons necessary for service of coffee and tea will be supplied in laying the cover, but, if necessary, they can be laid on the saucers as the cups are taken or passed to the individual guest.

An After-Dinner Coffee Service of Portsmouth Pattern

The Demi-Tasse

WITH after-dinner coffee, the waitress should pass loaf sugar with silver tongs, and, if the guests desire it, cream also should be offered, though after-dinner coffee is supposed to be taken black.

If it is desired, the demi-tasse may be served with the cheese and crackers. After dinner, coffee may be served in the drawing-room, the waitress passing the cups on a tray, each guest helping himself.

Smoking-service

AFTER the formal dinner, when the ladies have retired to the drawing-room, cigars and cigarettes are offered to the gentlemen. These may be brought to table in the cedar-lined silver boxes which accompany many smoking-sets.

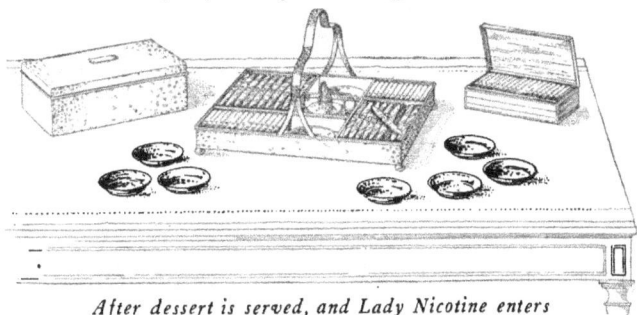

After dessert is served, and Lady Nicotine enters
The cigarette and cigar service

"THE feast now done, discourses are renewed,
  And witty arguments with mirth pursu'd;
  The cheerful master mid his jovial friends,
  His glass to their best wishes recommends.
  The grace-cup follows to his sovereign's health
  And to his country plenty, peace and wealth.
  Performing then the piety of grace,
  Each man that pleases reassumes his place."

Dr. King, "The Art of Cookery,"
London, 1740.

How to Serve Afternoon Tea

TEA service is rapidly becoming a factor around which our social and domestic life revolves. Tea gives an opportunity for the exercise of an hospitality that adds grace to our every-day life, and the tea table becomes the synonym for simple and agreeable entertaining.

The tea-wagon, or table with its service of silver, the glistening kettle, the attractive cups, the dainty

For Afternoon Tea
A touch of charming hospitality

service of small cakes or brown crisp toast, either cinnamon-spread or simply and daintily buttered, the tempting little sandwich,—all add to the delight and pleasure of the group.

The rules for the service of tea are few; formality is absent, the pleasure great, good cheer and friendliness the outcome.

Silver Tea-pot
Colonial Boston, seventeenth century

A hostess usually asks some of her friends to assist her by pouring tea, service for which is at one end of a long table. This service should consist of a regular silver tea-service with china cups and plates, napkins, etc. When tea is poured, sugar or lemon is added according to the preference of the person served. A teaspoon is placed upon the

saucer beside the cup of tea. Two or three silver
trays should be upon the table, each containing sugar,
sugar-tongs, cream, and dish with silver inset containing slices of lemon. Sand-
wiches and cakes are passed by
friends of the hostess.

It is the duty of the waitress, or
some member of the family acting
as such, to remove the cups and
spoons, bringing others to replace
them and to replenish the supplies of sandwiches and cakes.

First of all, let the water be
bubbling boiling—more than
steaming hot. Let it sing its solo
in the kettle. Then, with tea-pot
freshly scalded and shining hap-
pily, let the tea be put in—a teaspoon of tea for each cup to be
served and always one for the pot.
Pour the bubbling, boiling water
over the tea, let it stand for a mo-
ment, merely that. It will then
be sufficiently infused to give a
delicate, perfect cup of tea. When
more tea is required, infuse more.
It is a simple process.

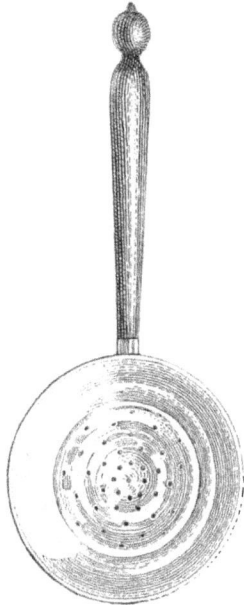

Silver Strainer
For tea or other bever-
ages; early Colonial.
Sturdy, ample, and useful

Offer with the cup of tea, as it
is presented, sugar and cream, or, if preferred,
lemon, thinly sliced, and sugar to suit the taste of
the guest. Present the small cakes neatly arranged
on plates, the toast, napkin covered on a tray, and
the sandwiches, comfortably stacked on plates.

So proceeds a simple tea, an expression of delightful hospitality.

The Cup of Tea

"Now stir the fire and close the shutter fast,
  Let fall the curtains, wheel the sofa round,
And, when the bubbling and loud hissing urn
  Throws up a steamy column, and the cups
That cheer, but not inebriate, wait on each,
  So let us welcome peaceful evening in."

—Cowper.

A Water Service of Silver, of Southern Colonial Type
Note the interesting lines of the silver goblets, the pride of the
hostess, and a charming expression of Southern hospitality

When the Weather is Hot

ICED tea and coffee should come directly from
the serving pantry and be supplied in tall glasses
upon small glass plates. To each guest at the time
of serving the waitress also supplies a long-handled
silver spoon.

Tall glasses containing iced tea are decorated with
slices of lemon. These may be cut so they can be

slipped over the rim of the glass. Garnishes of mint and lemon verbena are pleasant additions to the lemon. After these have been served, the waitress should supply each guest with soft sugar, and cream, if desired, and she should be watchful to supply more cracked ice for the glasses, if necessary.

Tea and Coffee

FILLED cups of tea or coffee served with meals may come directly from the kitchen, in which case the waitress offers to each guest, after she has served the cup, loaf sugar with silver tongs, and cream; and in the case of tea, sliced lemon as well.

The hostess may serve from a tea-wagon, if desired.

COFFEE

COFFEE, which makes the politician wise
And see through all things with his half-shut eyes.
—Pope, "Rape of the Lock."

A dignified service of Etruscan pattern

BIBLIOGRAPHY

Historical

1. "Country Contentments or English Housewife"
   Gervaise Markham, London, 1623

2. "The Whole Duty of a Woman, or an Infallible
   Guide to the Fair Sex"
   London, 1737

3. "Antiquitates Culinariæ, or Curious Tracts"
   Richard Warner, London, 1791

4. "The Court and Country Cook"
   Translated out of French into English by J. K.,
   London, 1702

5. "Scenes and Characters of the Middle Ages"
   Edward L. Cutts, London, 1872

6. "The Accomplished Cook"
   Robert May, London, 1678

7. "Queens of England"
   Agnes Strickland, London, 1847

8. "Shakespeare's England," 2 vols.
   G. W. Thornbury, London, 1856

9. "History of Domestic Manners and Sentiments
   in England during the Middle Ages"
   Thomas Wright, Esq., M.A., F.S.A., London, 1862

BIBLIOGRAPHY—*continued*

Historical

10. "A Book about the Table"
     John Cordy Jeaffreson, London, 1875

11. "Shakespeare's England"
     Oxford University Press, 1917

12. Chaucer's "England," Vol. I
     Matthew Brown, London, 1869

13. "Domestic Life in Scotland, 1488–1688"
     John Warrack, New York, 1919–20

Modern

1. "Practical Cooking and Dinner Giving"
    Mrs. Mary F. Henderson, New York, 1876–1904

2. "The American Waiter"
    John B. Goins, Chicago, 1914

3. "Home Economics"
    Maria Parloa, New York, 1910